Rasa

Joanne Dominique Dwyer

Marsh Hawk Press • 2022
East Rockaway, New York

For
Paige Dominique Young
&
August Joseph Young

Take this longing from my tongue
All the useless things my hands have done
Let me see your beauty broken down
Like you would do for one you love

- Leonard Cohen

Cover photograph: Heidi Cost
Cover & Text design: Anna Reich

Marsh Hawk books are published by Marsh Hawk Press, Inc., a not-for-profit corporation
under section 501(c)3 United States Internal Revenue Code.

Library of Congress Cataloging-in-Publication Data
Names: Dwyer, Joanne Dominque, author.
Title: Rasa / Joanne Dominque Dwyer.
Description: First Edition. | East Rockaway, New York : Marsh Hawk Press, Inc., 2022.
Identifiers: LCCN 2021046207 | ISBN 9780996991278 (paperback)
Subjects: LCGFT: Poetry.
Classification: LCC PS3604.W92 R37 2021 | DDC 811/.6--dc23
LC record available at https://lccn.loc.gov/2021046207

Marsh Hawk Press
P.O. Box 206, East Rockaway, N.Y. 11518-0206
mheditor@marshhawkpress.org

SONG OF SAP

At dawn, a hummingbird orbiting my skull
      as if I were a flower.

As if I bled nectar!

Trying to sense if I could be trusted to land upon.

Spillage from my crown chakra, like a cloud
      that cannot keep hold of secrets.

Rasa is the almond scent of bones leaning into each other
      to forge a sealed door.

The ambergris in the intestines of whales, altar of rose, vapor trail.

Grains of rice infused in milk and musk.

One day our skull bones will open again – unhinged
      by crowbar – or a barely audible breeze.

Only a sensitive spectator might take this journey with me.

There will be waist-high drifts of snow;
      a warehouse full of wedding gowns.

Rasa is the ruby in a bloodshot eye; the lily in the lungs of a girl.

At dusk, a hummingbird circling my barren garage ceiling –
      like an a plane waiting out a storm.

CONTENTS

Black Sun

Chaperone   7

So, You Think I'm Afraid of You?   8

Cult of the White Bear   10

S Dnem Rozhdeniya, Leo Tolstoy   12

Handsome Is as Handsome Does   14

Re-Entry   16

Some Kind of Bird   18

Semi-Jubilant Conversion Song   20

To Charette With a Man   23

Sin   26

When Almonds Appear in Dreams   28

Shining Bucket   30

Man With Machete   32

Saint of Storms

Shallow Person   36

Tarzan Aubade   38

Desperate Escapee   40

Burial Customs   42

Dream on a Dead Painter's Birthday   44

Patron of Embalmers   46

Autostrada of the Lakes   48

Seven Valleys   50

Lead in the Boots of the Messengers   53

Marble   55

Levels of Lead   56

Fractured Light

Miracle of Life   60

Trajectory of the Sun   62

No Alphabet   64

Invidia   66

Dialogue of the Deaf   68

Color-Ridden   70

Inside the Jiva of a Madwoman   72

Decline in the Adoration of Jack-in-the-Pulpits   74

Post Scriptum: I Don't Drive Tractors   76

Riding With No Hands   78

Gracias Anselmo   80

Black Sun

CHAPERONE

To keep watch. Not my indigo eye on the ball

nor in the blacklight peephole.

Not on the blisters dappling my feet.

Nor on the beauty or the ugly in the mirror.

But on the children in the playground and on the fur-matted squirrels.

From a wooden tower, the running herds.

From the leaning alabaster lighthouse, a one-armed mermaid

out-swimming the divers, with tanks on their backs,

chasing her, like erasers of magic.

Eye on the bird, that its head does not hit glass.

On the sky, for the sun's second coming, though she

might have been inebriated when she swore to return.

My small room smelling like canned tuna fish in oil.

My dry cough keeping both of us awake.

Chaperone: *The supervision of vulnerable women in public spaces.*

A shepherd is a chaperone.

Neruda asking *What do they call the sadness of a solitary sheep?*

Derived from the French word for a hood or cape.

Covering the eyes of a prisoner.

And the children sinking in the winter mud needed rescue.

I was a child sinking in winter mud and needed rescue.

And someone did come and grab my wrists.

SO, YOU THINK I'M AFRAID OF YOU?

I'm not afraid of you or the black sun.
Not afraid of the colony of ants in my floorboards
or the displaced people sleeping in my treehouse.
I'm not afraid of the rain depluming the clothes from my skin
as it pelts down hard as hail, hard as a hammer, hard as the shell
of a musk turtle overturned and unable to right itself.
Not afraid of the dove-colored smoke moving in the air
in the pattern of a cry for help; in the pattern of waving goodbye.
Not afraid to be ejected from the opera house for singing
along to the aria about the woman about to hang herself
because her lover won't convert to her family's religion.
Or perhaps she is dying of scarlet fever.
A friend today saying *Crazy how the venom stays in the body for days*
referring to a Tabaño fly bite on her foot.
I'm not afraid of drinking a bottle of tainted Tabasco sauce
or of diving into a gelid and storm-tossed ocean
where the only people on the beach are lovers
sequestered in the sand dunes far enough away
that they would never hear my cries for help.
It's hard enough to ask a stranger for jumper cables
or a neighbor to water your lawn, in case of severe drought,
while you go away for a few weeks to fat camp
in hopes of coming home thinner. Some men
are tender and say *it just means there is more of you to love.*
Other men are managerial and say *Don't eat ___! and don't eat ___!*
Others have a swaggering fallacious sense of empathy
and offer *How about I drive alongside you in my truck*
while you huff it around the block four or five times?

While driving, they are listening to the radio, downing beers,

eating pork rinds and ranch-flavored corn nuts with the heater on,

as you jog in threadbare shoes, in the frigid air, like someone being

relocated, forced to traverse for days across a Trail of Tears.

But that is an opera in progress, requiring animal hides.

I'm not afraid of progress; it's just that I see so little of it.

And I will understand you calling me out

for using the Trail of Tears in a way that diminishes

the devastation it was for those who walked it.

And for those who starved, froze, bled-out along the way.

I'm not afraid to apologize for that.

I'm not afraid to tell you that it's physically impossible

for a pig to raise its head to the sky.

CULT OF THE WHITE BEAR

What do we know about the man who said *The union*
of souls is a thousand times more beautiful than that of bodies?
We know his name was Ibn Hazm
and he was born in Cordoba, Spain in 994
under the sky of a scorpion –
and he believed women could be prophets.

A much slower propagation of propaganda before the printing press.
A much closer view of the night constellations
before massive flood lights and the headlamps of miners.
What do we know about the hearts of salamanders?
And the headlights of trucks carrying coconuts
and papayas from Panama to the Arctic Circle
where we know close to nothing about the Cult of the White Bear.

We know among the Nivkh, the bear festival
is an inter-clan ceremony, where the clan of the wife-takers
restores ties with the clan of the wife-givers.
We know some Mormon fundamentalist sects
are sick mother-fuckers, garrotters of girls.
And Utah residents use more Prozac,
to raise serotonin levels, than the residents
of any other state in the U.S.

We know shot glasses and snow globes
are accepted souvenirs.
We know the scorpion constellation above us
serves as a cue to curtail our excessive pride.
And sometimes poison is the only cure.
But be careful about dyeing your hair
repeatedly and over a lifetime,
especially in the color of a sable.

We know not to light up a cigarette
near to Aunt Margaret and the papoose
of an oxygen tank she carries like a child
she will never drop off at a summer camp
to learn the art of archery
and edible plant identification.
A child she hordes, the way
others amass lamp oil
and 5 gallon jugs of potable water.

S DNEM ROZHDENIYA, LEO TOLSTOY

Leo Tolstoy, today is your 189th birthday.

It's Indian summer, and the allergens and pilgrimages have shushed.

Lawn chairs remain in the yard yellowing the slow-dying grass underneath

as birds are shaping themselves into arabesques in the apricot trees.

I prize your protracted life and how you could be God's doppelganger

with your long beard like a hundred snakes lined up side by side for a firing squad.

Though no one has sighted you lately sitting in a booth at a truck stop restuarant

or banging a drum under a thicket of willows outside of Norman, Oklahoma,

you still stand as vertical as the claret-colored bricks of a crematorium chimney;

only use a cane when swatting at astral spirits.

It is said that meeting a chimney sweep by chance will bring a person luck.

We know Marilyn's luck changed drastically after singing *Happy Birthday, Baby.*

But what fortune I feel in having a Leo moon in my astrological chart

even if it pegs me as jealous and prone to sulking.

I like to fantasize that with you at my side, Leo Tolstoy,

in a Russian blizzard or on the scalding sands of the Black Sea in summer

that I would no longer be a malcontent.

Though, I confess how akin I am to your Anna K.

How inclined I am to ruining love,

the way she was prone to ruining love,

sabotaging it like a bread mold razes a loaf of rye.

Women like she and I know the nomenclature of extinct species

and the names of nightshades, but it's near-impossible

for us to believe that we measure up to any love

besides a canary's or a dog's love for the one who feeds it.

Leo, you stopped eating braised loin of veal, and then your estate's eggs,
but could not stop yourself from dreaming of mice.
The way it's so much easier to love a fabled sea monster
or the woman standing on her head in the sepia photo
than to love the flesh and blood man at my side.
Though, recently I had a little change of luck.
I had been incrementally falling out of love with a man.
But then he mercy-killed my ailing chicken,
didn't skimp on the depth of the hole he dug to bury it,
vacuumed my car really well and for a very long time,
even though there was a playoff game on television.
And my deleterious descent into Eros began all over again.

HANDSOME IS AS HANDSOME DOES

My mother has the name of a goddess and was on a game
show sometime in the 1970's. She came home with a barrel.

That was her winnings: a barrel that opened up into a bar.
If you ever find yourself on a game show, remember incest

not cannibalism, was the first taboo. Though this is not
the case with gibbons. A gibbon father deprived of his wife

will mate with his daughter, and a widowed mother with her
son. Don't you hate that everything gets turned into a symbol?

As in the Crucifixion is symbolic of castration. And a second
toe longer than a big toe indicates one is emotionally tame.

And Freud saying *Sometimes a cigar is just a cigar*, yet he saw
the stalks of white asparagus and the shed feathers of pheasants

as phallic. And a handsome surgeon does not guarantee
he or she won't leave a sponge inside you. And just because

someone is good-looking, it doesn't mean they are safe to
travel with. Case in point: there is a genus of water beetle

with the godlike name Hydrodessus, where the males suffocate
the females underwater, in order to make them submissive to sex.

And lately there have been eyewitness reports of the recent
phenomenon of elephants raping rhinoceroses, so be prepared

if the game show host asks: Does the world need more elephant
psychologists, elephant crucifixions, or elephant castrations?

Whack the buzzer rapidly and reply: The world could use a new hero,
not necessarily handsome, to chimney-sweep the collective unconscious.

And just because he was handsome, my mother should not have brought the
game show host home. Nor should she have fed him waffles in the morning.

RE-ENTRY

Be it a white porcelain bathtub or the Red Sea, some of us are afraid of water.
Others are afraid of eating uncooked meat, of spending our lives tethered
like balloons to dialysis machines or unwanted partners.

At dawn, I spy a rare blue-collared dove on the rim of the birdbath
reminiscent of an Egyptian queen stoic in a falling rain.
For most of us the feathered creature is beauty incarnate.

For my fiancé, it conjures a flashback of his father dove-hunting with a large rifle
not in forest, but in a city park resplendent with heroic statues, old men playing
chess, teenagers skateboarding, toddlers taking their first steps.

Instead of disentangling myself from the son of a depraved dove-hunter, knowing
some pasts cannot be recovered from, I track down recipes in an out-of-print
French country cookbook for Dove Breast, Dove Stroganoff and Doves on Toast.

I cook these entrees over three consecutive Thursdays, but am unable to eat the birds.
For doves are disemobodied souls resting in sawdust, mascots for pacifists
and militants, companions of Aphrodite.

It's psychedelic, that one minute we are under the spell of being spun, blindfolded holding a paper donkey tail in our little hairless hands, whirling, as if we are inside a benevolent wind, and the next moment we are in a welting, vision-impairing rain.

Then lying alone on a raft in the eye of the storm, as if anesthetized on a surgical table. And though no one has uppercut me in years – I'm still afraid of stairs, of being stepped on, of cherries.

SOME KIND OF BIRD

Odysseus built his wife Penelope a bed.

One of the four legs of the bed was a live olive tree.

We all want to be loved in that manner – in the way

of a fixed bridal bed, nothing on wheels or deflatable.

Like an ancillary Odysseus, my grandfather was a longshoreman –

loading and unloading cargo in a stationary NYC harbor.

He wanted me named Penelope.

And a tether is a rope or a chain used to tie

an animal, to restrict its movements.

Like the way my brother was tethered

to the garage door as a toddler, so that our

mother might read her magazines in frictionless repose

and her son might learn the art of delayed gratification.

Constrained like a young bull building hatred

for the matadors and picadors to come.

Maybe that's how my brother later survived being held hostage –

tied up and gagged in the back of his small jeep

for trying to buy crack with no money.

The story goes that my grandfather barged into the small seaside

hospital to say I was born on St. Penelope's Day

and that I would be cursed if not given her name.

My grandfather died while drinking a cup of tea in the kitchen with his wife.

Penelope is a stand-in for marital faithfulness.

The opposite of an illicit reservoir swim

and an echoing turquoise-colored Taos hotel room.

Some say her name is pre-Greek

and means some kind of bird.

Others note that elops is a suffix for migratory

animals – so close to *elope*.

I cannot find a St. Penelope in any official canon of saints.

And so few civilizations bury their dead sitting up.

I don't have a single item of my grandfather's:

not a Sunday shirt, a soup thermos, or a shoehorn.

Consigned to our graves shoeless

to deter and handicap our spirits from

wandering and roaming distances in the new dark.

Though, of late, burial slippers

are coming back in vogue.

One size fitting all.

SEMI-JUBILANT CONVERSION SONG

God can be located   in the candied red syrup
of Grenadine   &   in the gunpowder of a grenade.

In the ocean breeze scenting the black hair
of a woman combing the beach for colored glass –

and in the stale air in a stalled elevator shaft.

God resides in the feathered head of a falcon –

     and in the hour-old embryo of a child
   conceived during a one-night stand.

Say you want a revolution –
     It's not too late to convert your way of thinking to my way of thinking.

Say you missed the Easter egg hunt the year your pelvis
    broke open like a watermelon –

and you watched the other children from your bed
      through antique opera glasses

your father bought your mother on eBay.

    Watched them scurrying around like a family of thirsty quail –
or delirious mud-caked crusaders.

All of Muhammad's sons died in infancy.

And Fatima was his only daughter
who did not precede him in death.

An eclipse of the sun followed the funeral
of one of his cradled sons.
And though Muhammad
declared *The light does not darken for anyone's death* –
even savants are savaged
by such an avalanche of loss.

Say you want to have a party for God, but you're not sure
he likes blood sausage –
can tolerate lactose or loud hypnotic sound waves.

It dawns on you, that you really don't know him.
Don't know what his stance is on food stamps or liposuction.

If he prefers androgynous women –
or women who wear curlers in their hair to the supermarket.
If he's drawn to men who carve miniature wooden animals
or men who climb poles for a living.

If he regrets creating us in a palette of colors.

And it dawns on you that you often feel

like burning yourself at the stake.

But somehow you know that while God
is idle of late, sitting in the sun for hours
playing the pennywhistle –

eventually he will rise up
from the singed-blue buffalo grass, pull the wedgie
from his ass

and accept our invitations
to swim across the light-pervious lake together.

TO CHARETTE WITH A MAN

It's June and a woman is traveling alone on an airplane
soaring over a vast ocean. She tells a stranger

that this is her first trip to Paris in order to
charette with a man. She doesn't share with the

stranger that she and the man met eight months
earlier at a biker bar in the states, on September 23 –

the death date of both Freud and Neruda.
Freud of buccal cancer: *relating to, or forming part of the cheek.*

Neruda of heart failure.
Children are taught not to talk to strangers

nor to be coerced by candy into the trunks of cars.
To charette is to meet to map out a solution.

It is also a chariot or cart used to transport drawings.
A collaborative session of walking up pyramidic steps

to see the hairbrushes and dried-up umbilical cords
of saints laid out on faded red velvet.

Without the chic black leather jacket the woman accidentally
left hanging on the bathroom door at the Heathrow airport

because she was more occupied with changing her underwear
in anticipation of seeing the man, she is cold in the evenings

and when it rains. She considers buying a new leather jacket
in one of the tiny sheepskin shops in the white

mountain village but is afraid the man she
came to meet will judge her as capricious

with her possessions. She is even self-conscious to
purchase a soy chai from the Paris Starbucks

as if to do so would mark her as infirm, her body
echoing an insatiable choir of hunger and thirst.

Since the man is a psychologist, they hunt rare book shops
along *Rue de la Bucherie* for signed copies of Freud.

The man agrees with Freud that orgasms escort
one to the annihilation of the self, which in turn

leads to a thrice-happy assimilation into God. Be it
a God who makes his living as a hermetic fur trapper

or an ungoverned hapless God napping, fly unzipped
spittle trolling onto his beard, near the Seine.

Walking back to their hotel in the rain, the man
and the woman agree the solution is not to marry.

Back in the States, the woman hears credible evidence
that Neruda may have been murdered.

There's talk of exhuming his remains –
to estrange breadgrain from his body,

and to pull his body back from the beauty of botany.

Neruda is the poet she likes to read
at other people's weddings:

I hate you deeply, and hating you /bend to you.

SIN

Sin is the name of a moon god that chaperons over long tracks of sky –

not the punishable act that causes one to shrink in size

and doggie-paddle in the murk-ridden waters of regret.

It's likely the goats in the orchard will survive with

or without circumcisions or bells around their necks.

And despite all of our marvelous infractions, it's unlikely that

an otherworldly scroll exists with our names on it.

And how heroic sounding that *Sin had a beard*

made of lapis lazuli and rode a winged bull.

And how viripotent that Sin

fathered both the Sun and Venus.

In a bar my friend tells my man she likes his beard.

On the cover of this month's New Yorker

Botticelli's Venus arrives on a Long Island beach

and everyone on the sand takes out their smartphones

and circles her like a swarm of paparazzi –

or a bale of snapping turtles.

Hardly anyone sees the world through naked eyes anymore –

or scans the sky for Arctic terns.

No one cuts out coupons or wax-seals letters.

Some still hand-stitch skirts for their daughters

with the hope that some son of a prosperous god might

stare open-mouthed at their daughter's stunning asymmetry

and buy her a beachside condo and an Audi with airbags.

The other day my daughter asked the beauteous Vietnamese man

giving her a manicure if he dreamed in Vietnamese or English.

He smiled in such a way that made me think

no one had ever asked him that question before.

Hardly any of us soaking in Epson salt baths

or capsizing in boats anymore.

Hardly any of us baking bread

without a bread-making machine.

Or mulching our fruit trees

with unhostility and love before winter.

WHEN ALMONDS APPEAR IN DREAMS

When almonds appear in dreams
they foreshadow a temporary sorrow.

Like old dresses and orthopedic shoes boxed
in the cellar like crates of pressed cider

or a bell rung in the late afternoon.

Like the old folks fed at 5 pm, drugged at 6 pm –
made as still as empty bird baths.

They say if a woman dreams of a glass jar of jellybeans
she will narrowly escape electrocution.

And if she dreams her hair is the shade of the sky
in a summer storm, her child will be stillborn.

Intimacy means profoundly interior –
countless sets of keys and cryptic codes.

Jogging along the train tracks, I come across
mammoth yellow machinery with colossal tires

and a dark-skinned surveyor
whose gender I cannot decode.

I often don't care if my facts are verifiable
or if the winter hens lay less eggs.

It is said a gapped-tooth man will die of tuberculosis.
And do not lean a broom against a bed.

And a wart on your neck means you will be hanged.
Superstitions are said to be irrational

but I say beware of a man who posts his IQ
on his dating profile and boasts

of never having swung at a piñata.
It's so much more sagacious to date a boardwalk

sketch artist who sits in a portable chair
in paint-stained jeans and flip-flops

and though he is severely allergic to the sea air
and to paper cuts, he renders all of his subjects

with either the exaggerated symmetry
of sex kittens or prizefighters.

SHINING BUCKET

To heave-ho water from the well in a shining bucket.
For fear to lift, from the lake, like ribbon lightning.

People take flight from excessive lies, but not everyone with ringworm
of the foot is athletic, nor loves the clang of a banging shining bucket.

To lift fingerprints from the salt and pepper shakers, from the
helicopter blade, from the lion's mane in a shining bucket.

And a Munchausen's-by-Proxy mother in a shining
bucket can be a blessing if you hate gym class.

An adaptor coupling adheres two separate shafts
for the purpose of transmitting power in a shining bucket.

The he/he, she/she, he/she pairing up, the side by side all-aboard
of the ark. The two-for-one meal coupon in a shining bucket

at Long John Silver's. The pirate's leg sawed off close to the hip;
a parrot on his shoulder eating seed in a shining bucket.

Princess Di stuck her finger down her throat in a shining bucket.
And the press reports that Sarah Palin and the princess are 10th cousins

and both telegenic in a shining bucket. Meaning looking good
on television. A 10th cousin is someone who is descended

from the brother or sister of your great, great, great, great,
great, great, great, great, great grandparent in a shining bucket.

And *the one who cracks-up is drowning in the same water
in which the mystic swims* in a shining bucket.

See the couple, spavined as old race horses
shuttering the windows on an infernal afternoon

lying in bed next to each other, opting
to leave their bodies, in one shining bucket.

MAN WITH MACHETE

Have you ever come back into consciousness
to a cannibal song chorused
into your ear by a hungering ghost?
Or been sung to sleep by someone at your side
rather than by a cassette tape?
With equal force, they will devour you
if you open your curtain too wide.
Limos is the goddess of starvation.
I'm not sure why Limousines impress people
or how they got to be status symbols –
ferrying the backseat squatters to gushy galas
and Madison Square Garden to see the Ice Capades,
without having to be fretful about parking or the rain.
As if drinking champagne in the back
of the elongated car means you will never die.
Except, before I even exit the limo, my stockings have run
and I have fallen out of love with the man sitting next to me.
And seeing Yogi Bear on ice skates will only make me homesick
for mornings in my pajamas eating red licorice, with no hint of death.

And no premonition that years later I will voyage south
and be woken by the megaphoned voice of a man selling shrimp
from his battered pickup on the potholed roads behind the sea;
feel a euphoric sense of belonging when I stumble
upon the town's burial grounds abundant with brazenly
colored floral bouquets and prepossessed plastic saints.
And close to twilight, while jogging alone in the jungle
I come upon a man carrying a machete.
He is built like a Toro Bravo bull,
has the vast scar of a Titian-red centipede
slashed across his face, as if he might have
disfigured himself as well as others with the blade.
His eyes black as a sheet of tar paper.
A tattoo of the *Virgen de Guadalupe* on his throat –
more exquisite than any strand of diamonds.

Saint of Storm

SHALLOW PERSON

What if I were not a shallow person.

Did not need honey in my mouth.

Did not need a handsome man to motivate me to shower.

What if I was able to mimic an aviary bird,

could hide all signs of injury;

did not spend hours making rubber band balls.

What if I could dress in a color-coordinated manner,

did not need opiates to talk to you.

What if I were backseat enough

to never need to say another word.

Unpossessive enough to let someone

without vocal cords and a tongue have mine.

What if the African continent lifted up from the earth

and travelled like a magic carpet, landing on North America,

smothering the USA as if it were putting out a fire.

And the African continent liked its new home,

did not mind being a continent on top of another continent,

did not mind hearing all the dead below it crying

out for their fields of leveled corn and smashed swing sets.

Some of us begging for lamb shish kabobs,

others of us moaning for tofu and kale smoothies.

What if I never wore a cast or swallowed cough syrup.

And Caspian tigers were not extinct.

And chrysanthemums levitated.

What if I stopped whitening my teeth,

pitched a tent in your backyard, propagated violets and cacti.

Did not need a communion wafer

or the tongue of a man in order to feel inhabited.

What if I was ordinary enough to ride the bus;

eat microwave dinners.

What if I had been brave enough the day the sun

bore its heat down on us, browning our scalps

as we swatted away horseflies and hornets –

to have run Uncle Bob over with the tractor

instead of unwittingly masticating

a den of newborn rabbits.

TARZAN AUBADE

It's never a good sign when the patron saint
of betrothed couples is also the patron saint of the plague.
Nor is it a sign that things are looking up
when you put vodka in your water bottle.
Or eat a whole bag of Cheetos before 6 am
all the while over-ingesting the orange dye
knowing it has to do with how much you miss Tarzan
and the deep sadness you feel because he has a stress fracture
in his right foot and can no longer play tennis with you.

It's never an auspicious sign when on Valentine's Day
the ocean side restaurant is out of the catch-of-the-day.
But you make good with baba ganoush as Tarzan eats quail.
And it's never a happy portent when other women, and a few
men stare at your date's loincloth, though it means they are
diverted away from the ochre stains on your mouth.

The Spanish word for naked is *desnudo*
and *pelado* is a man with a shaved head –
or a landscape empty of trees.
A sentence without a period is simply unpunctuated
but does not resemble a punctured lung.

It's never a reassuring sign when your child
prefers the company of cats over humans
or finger-paints scenes of decapitation in kindergarten.
Nor is it a couleur de rose sign when you have panic attacks
at the thought of someone brushing your hair
or you are drawn to trading places
with someone wearing a lab coat.

It's far from a promising sign when you telephone
a dominant or a submissive for hire
on the fire escape in the dark
during a major holiday with your family in earshot.
Or when you wake at dawn after dreaming
of licorice and amputated limbs
and you see a woman out the window
traversing through the snowy meadow wearing a ruby knit hat.
You can't tell if she's carrying a harpoon
in her hand or a broken cross-country ski.
If she's running away or towards.

DESPERATE ESCAPEE

There's a lone man manacled in handcuffs
   on the side of the highway. As petrified as an opal.

Eyes like the melancholic eyes of a fish dying in a bucket
   or the unhinged eyes of a young man plummeting through the air.

Half-vanished into the shadow cast by pinon trees;
   half-exposed in dappled sunlight, gesturing for a ride.

And just as the four directions each has a distinctive
   scent and disposition, texture and length of hair –

ways of ambulating and supplicating, sometimes akin to ants
   or the excommunicated, there are four types of people.

The first flips the manacled man a finger and calls
   the authorities with the escapee's precise GPS location.

The second pretends not to see the man and hums
   a little louder to a Tammy Wynette song on the radio.

The third pulls over, rolls down the window the width of an
   atrophied arm bone, then changes her mind and speeds off,

but twenty feet away, slows down again, just long enough to
   toss out a bag of corn chips and a small carton of chocolate milk.

The fourth type stops close to the pinon trees, gets out
   and motions for the manacled man to get inside the car.

The earliest hand-restraints were fastened from strips of animal hide.
   In the fourth century BCE, there were sightings of chariots

piled high with primitive handcuffs – belonging to some
     army travelling south in anticipation of collecting captives.

And just as I've never fenced or chained a dog, I've never
     manacled a man to the wrought-iron filigree of my bed.

For what can come of a love without
     the full consent to act without constraint?

All of us with the idée fixe for our lives to end
     with red ribbons and black swans in a wind.

And for this story to end with the escapee
     entering the back of a little dented red hatchback

and lying under the faux Sioux patterned blanket
     stored in the car in case of a blizzard

as the car drives further south, beyond the billboards
     advertising accident attorneys and outlet malls

to where pasture lands expand, dogs are landloping;
     children are lovingly ungroomed –

and welders keep an assortment of acetylene
     torches shaded under their tin-roofed shops.

BURIAL CUSTOMS

When a man, woman or child dies in Indonesia, a sacrificial
    water buffalo carries their soul into the afterlife.

Rather than down a tree to make a coffin, South Sea Islanders
    bury their dead in standing hollowed-out tree trunks.

Often the tree selection begins when a person gets sick.
    In South Korea, they are running out of land to lay-to-rest

their dead, so human remains are made into gem-like glass beads
    in the colors of turquoise, pink and black –

displayed in brass bowls in family living rooms.
    If one dies in New Orleans, the melancholic music turns raucous

once you're in the ground, and it's acceptable to wear thick eyeliner
    and a palette of dazzling colors on your cheeks and lips

whether you're one of the mourners or the one in the coffin.
    For it's wise to look mesmerizing and eye-catching

and not completely disconsolate and torn-apart
    when arriving on the other side. The sacred texts

of Islam say the dead are to be buried in the soil
    but Allah will sanction a sea burial if there's a chance

an enemy will dig up your body in order to mutilate it.
    Filipinos blindfold their dead and sit them down

in a chair made of sugarcane outside the entrances of their homes
    and place unlit cigarettes in their mouths.

Whether we arrive on the back of a beautiful beast
    or are transported inside the sap-moist skin of a tree

those that greet us on the other side will be the ones
    we will ask to borrow a needle and thread –

the ones who will tell us where to forage wild lettuce
    where to re-sole our boots, the ones

to offer us a sex toy if our sorrow is unbearable.
    On TV, I heard Joseph Campbell say

the god of sex is also the god of death.
    I also heard an Indian sadhu say *Reflect*

that someday you will suddenly leave this world,
    so it's best to make the acquaintance of God now.

I'd like to have tea and apricot crepes with God
    comb the hyenas from his hair –

for him to comb the labyrinth from mine.
    I'd like to not fear the hidden, have no need

of certainty, not be afraid to be buried naked
    without a cell phone or a pet at my side.

DREAM ON A DEAD PAINTER'S BIRTHDAY

Morning after morning
    my man sits in bed staring
        into the yawning abyss of his iPad.

        I've just returned from my nightly visit in the altar-world
            where cotton candy is the main nourishment,
                no one's hair gets knotted, and all doors lead to an audience with God.

            I tell my man I dreamt of a man with worms in his ear.
          The man's head lay in my lap heavy as an ostrich egg in its nest.
       My hands evicting the helminths, white as lies, spawned from a bath of bleach,
                more maggot than worm.

Removing the delirium of waxen worms,
    I notice the absence of an entrance into the man's ear.
        Ousted or not, the worms would never materialize

      into his *milieu intérieur*, but forever mark time
          in that small ear saucer of skin, circling like newborn
              blind and hairless ferrets, corybantic for their mother's teat.

          Or a woman looking for a lipstick, a small piece of paper
        with something written on it – what she can't remember.
     Searching in the vacuous unlit cave of her vegan leather purse
          for a breath mint, a hairclip, an anodyne.

Long-whiskered owlets are dying.
    My man says I had the dream of the man with worms in his ears
        because it's Van Gogh's birthday.

A fact / *fait accompli* he has learned from his iPad.
I calculate the painter's gâteau would have required 166 candles today.
I imagine the colors of the wax sticks;

Vincent's hair close to the flames.
Jung said everything in the dream is you:
I am the man, the woman, the maggots.
One tires of the self as subject.

The largest flower on our planet, the corpse flower, is dying.
I wager Vincent knifed his ear, to silence auditory hallucinations.
Opposing understandings of grace.

I could dismember my man's electronic device.
Bury it in the military cemetery.
Or ride a horse at breakneck speed.

Wearing red beaver fur earmuffs
throughout the gallop.
I might be insanely cold or I might be seeking silence.

PATRON OF EMBALMERS

Depending on what staple sustenance was fed to you as a child –
beans, mustard greens, lamb balls in tamarind gravy

TV dinners on aluminum trays, each food group
in its own compartment, or candy dots on paper –

the souvenirs of excavations will either teeter-totter the drama
of your dreams, or teach you the tools of the forensic trade.

It goes without saying, the-sent-to-bed-without-dinner
will dream of platters of meat and melons. And the overstuffed will

dream of volcanoes and canoes. Freud believed dreams act as guardians
of our sleep, sentinels posted at the damp entrance of a dark tunnel –

though he felt contempt for philosophers and their futile word games.
It goes without saying that meanings fluctuate and multiplicity is desired

as in variety packs of little individual cereals
and sack as many women as you can.

At sixteen I was watching *The Exorcist* with my
Italian-American boyfriend in a movie theater just hours after

his schizophrenic brother, freshly-expelled from
the Rhode Island School of Design, came after us with a bat.

On screen the girl is confined to bed in a white nightgown
her head rotating faster than any planet around its sun.

If I had said The Patron Saint of Embroiderers,

how much softer would this soliloquy be?

Everyone knows well-fed children score higher on intelligence
tests and an embalmer is trained to forestall decomposition

and make the body suitable for public display.
In ancient Egypt, it involved levering open the mouth of a mummy

so the deceased could commence to eat ducks, lotuses
and leeks again in the afterlife.

Freud loved the boiled beef of Tafelspitz
but we don't know if he ate insects.

At eight years-old, in the middle of the night
he entered his parents' bedroom and urinated on their floor.

And his father declared *The boy will come to nothing.*
I have been accused of circumventing, and

though it sounds like a balmy breeze
billowing through the house, it means I

evade, avoid, skirt. I should have told
you straightaway that my movie date's name

was Paul Mecurio, and he was my first love.
And like his brother, he had a break –

and only an undersized trace of him
was ever found in a Florida everglade.

AUTOSTRADA OF THE LAKES

Sometime before I received numerous moving violations
from wide-shouldered cops wearing reflective sunglasses

on the Autostrada of the Lakes –
or spent time scheming as to how I could collect

SSI disability without deafening or impaling myself –
and before I had nursed my firstborn

on snow-capped and capitulating breasts,
I had slept with five different men, from five different continents.

Do you imagine a hashish addicted girl asleep on a bus station bench?
Or a long-skirted tambourine-shaking Hare Krishna devotee?

Or just a *femme moyen sensuel* who stole money
from her senile aunt for the journey?

And pledged to return when either her forehead
sunburned into the near-ecstasy of disfigurement

or the statute of limitations for her thievery expired.
Vanished and banished count as near-cousins in any coup.

None of the five men shared the same name,
yet all their names began with crushing consonants –

and the sibilant sound of a repeating rifle
aimed at herds of galloping horses.

None of the men loved their mothers,
so they only smiled when singeing the wings of insects.

I am told there were only two subjects in the Renaissance:
God and the fickleness of women.

And I too am being questioned. *Submit to the
black sounds*, said Lorca. Questioned as to whether

or not I can sleep in a state of starkness, with only
a kerosene lamp and an armless puppet as company.

Questioned as to whether or not I can
remain in one place long enough

to have my toe nails clipped or
to let anyone love me.

They all loved their mothers,
so they each wailed when I left.

Like the little boy in Giotto's *Ognissanti Madonna*
who cried each time his mother took him off

her lap and handed him back to the wet nurse
as soon as she was done posing for the painter.

And yes, each man had a flowered terrace.
Some sat and watched the sunset.

And yes, they all made sounds in the late afternoon,
that predated any alphabet.

SEVEN VALLEYS

Sounds like a retirement community with excavated lakes
    faux grass; a guard at the entrance sitting in a booth
        barring junky thieves, but waving exterminators through.

    Or the brand-name of the 300-count black sateen
bedsheets a bachelor buys for his circular bed.

The name of the sad little bedwetter
    walking like an injured inline skater
        to the door of his grandmother's bedroom
            in his soggy jungle animal pajamas, is not *Creator of Life-giving Water.*

Let's get this party started, said the tapper of the keg.

    And so said the Persian prophet, Baha'u'llah,
moments before our civil war, in which we threw engorged ashtrays
        and paper plates with oily taco meat at each other:
        Without dogma, we are like unbathed dogs.

And drink in this litany, in case you all lose sensation in your legs
    or you are sad 77% of the time:

I walk in the First Valley, in search of white rose soap
    to scour my heart hygienic, and a gypsum cave in which
        to leave behind my shoes.

I walk in the Second Valley of hero worship
     where carmine cactus flowers convince me
to fall in love with God, yet to see him
     as imperfect as a chainsaw without a chain.

I walk in the Third Valley of data and dossiers; learn
     knowledge is a hindrance –
          a dead fowl tied around my neck.

I walk in the Fourth Valley of unity
embarrassed by the blonde family at the airport
     wearing matching turquoise shirts
          advertising the fact that they reside
               below sea level.

I walk in the Fifth Valley of bodily acceptance
     on my way to the un-mirrored supermercado to buy aloe lotion
          for a sunburn received on a foreign mountain.

I walk in the Sixth Valley of wonderment
     because I don't know how the venom of a golden
          dart frog got in my throat and struck me mute
     liberating me from the obligation to small talk
with park rangers and parents at the bowling alley.

I end at the Seventh Valley
of Poverty and Absolute Nothingness.
The furthermost state any of us can attain
including a mystic or a wandering sadhu.

A place where your canteen has been punctured.

And God is wearing sweatpants, lying on a fainting couch
watching football with the sound off, as the sunset burns
neon as a liter of orange soda.

And I am kneeling on the indoor/outdoor carpet
beside him, pouring potato chips into a punch bowl

as our heads collide, like un-helmeted enemies –
as we both reach in.

.

.

LEAD IN THE BOOTS OF THE MESSENGERS

Late in the game I learn a throne is the moniker for an angel
of the seventh highest order, out of nine possible heights.

And those of us that suffer a dizzying vertigo must make peace with
bottom floor angels, bargain basement, *Everything's-On-Sale* angels.

A South American woman at the gym is wearing sweatpants
with the word Angel stenciled vertically down her leg.

She will not look me in the eye and is almost always breaking
the no-cell-phone rule, talking so heatedly, a la Latina,

while on the rowing machine. In the locker room, I am a voyeur
watching her blow-dry her hair, even in summer, when the sun

would do the same without injury. Her hair is as thin as a queen
ant's wing, which unfastens the instant it mates.

Because of the affinity between women, I've seen a windfall of breasts.
And recently I laid my eyes on the prototype of an adolescent Eve.

The most beauteous body coming out of a public shower.
A body that illuminated more than any library of books, cave

of echolocating bats or remnants of chandeliers. And I took in,
for the first time, the concupiscence of the old for the young.

And just as it is well past the era of electrocuting communists,
we are done seeing the snake as penis/messenger-boy of the devil.

The new symbology of the snake is exemplified in the revised creed
of the three R's: red lilies under a hypoallergenic pillow, a raspberry bruise,

and the unharnessed rappelling down the ravine without a reality show
there to film you. A willing, non-oppositional, *Come-to-Me Mama* dying.

And then the ingesting of our own death, as if death was an ostrich egg
or a fanny-pack full of trail mix that will get us up and over the

mountain pass, even in the deep snow, with fascists chasing us.
Yet, at the end of the adversity, after crossing the border,

we are reunited with our true loves or first childhood pets.
For the lucky, the two are one in the same and we wed soon after

our frostbite heals, but before a background check is run on us.
Though our betrotheds don't care that we were once strippers.

And most of our best work was choreographed in that era
when we were saturated of libations and libertine slogans

and sale underwear. And lead in the boots of the messengers
keeps them marching closer to the saltgrass, to the humidity of ants

and crushed beer cans. Look at the folded latticed wing
of a hibernating angel, just now unhinging its eyes, rising through

the air like caustic powdered sugar in the bakery warm from
the bread ovens. And though there are new forbidden fruits

and new machinery replacing red wheelbarrows;
truck drivers are still pulling off the road to sleep.

MARBLE

You are not the first person to stop loving me;
one marble in a factory of marbles.

The factory situated alongside a chemical-clouded river.
Crying fish are the reason the sea is salty.

A transitory truce flattens out the day like an opiate.
You are not the first person to believe soaking

in mineral salts will grant access into God's VIP lounge.
Jealousy is unswervingly sexual.

Though at times it's a neighbor's weathervane we covet.
Or a brass button adhered to a stranger's sweater.

Shall I deliver you an invitation to depart?
So you can catch the next train to another terrain:

a terrarium full of mouth-sutured women
wearing black ponchos.

What reason does a fish have for sorrow?
No longer offering up my night dreams to you;

I have scant waking ambition.
My infatuations are with color and form

and the chloroform of trance states;
the tiny paws of newborn snowshoe hares.

I'm not saying you aren't a beautiful marble.
I am saying the tattoos on my face are invisible.

LEVELS OF LEAD

When you say phone cord, I ideate it around my neck.
When you say I am alone in this mind of mine, I am not impaired
or lessened. When you say liquored-up, I conjure a Native man

riding a plastic horse. Or an estranged husband barbequing
in a backyard, recklessly liberal with the lighter fluid.
When you say the songbird dreams of singing

I hear the turquoise teakettle shrilling but am unable to tell
in what key because I don't lock the doors to my house.
I don't say home-invasion because it sounds so Homeland Security.

I don't say art is the lie that tells the truth, because I'm drawn
to fabulations and I've never sketched a harlequin or a dove
in number two pencils or red fingerpaint. Soap dries my hands

so I rarely use it. I don't say love redeemed from lust
because it echoes so evangelical and I don't believe
angels require bodyguards or tasters-of-their-food.

Someone tried to poison the president with a scrolled letter.
Two Chechen brothers blew up the marathon runners with
pressure cooker bombs. But if you were to say *Trust the water*

to hold you up, I might love you. But when you say
trope of loneliness, I say nothing is safe in the
suitcases of melancholics. And when you ask if I've

read Marquez's novella about an old man and a young girl
I say yes, but it made no impression on me or the levels of lead
in the soup bowls. When you ask what something elastic did

impress upon me, I say a mustard-grey haired man wearing
tan handyman coveralls in the dementia ward who told me
if I did not shut up, he would shut me up.

Fractured Light

MIRACLE OF LIFE

One of the abounding miracles of life on earth
is that somewhere at this moment a couple
is sitting in their backyard drinking alcohol together.
The lawn might be manicured or it might be overgrown
with Devil's Trumpet and Lantana weeds.
The backyard might belong to one of their elderly parents
who is lying in a darkened backroom watching television
as the couple imbibes India Pale Ale and mulberry wine.
Though maybe it's ethanol, because they just got
news they can't have children.
Or cartons of coconut water because
they just came back from the gym.
Regardless of what they are swallowing
and whether or not the backyard smells of cut grass
Asian barbeque or the pheromones of raccoons
together they are watching the stars enter the sky one by one
like teeth rising up into the gums of a toddler
as the crying sounds of mosquitoes and horseflies
being electrocuted in the iridescent bug zapper
over-occupies the atmosphere.

To the point that when the man says
Freud would find the above metaphorical reference
to teeth sexual, the woman can't quite hear him.
Instead she is contemplating the exacting way the man
lifts the beer bottle to his mouth, as if he is heralding
hound dogs through a horn; and about the way he
opened his car door last week for the neighbor woman
with olive skin and tattoos around her ankles
because she said her car wouldn't start
and she needed a ride into town
to return an overdue library book
and to euthanize her ferret.

TRAJECTORY TO THE SUN

The last time a guillotine was used to separate a head
    from a body of a human was in France in 1977.
His name was Hamida Djandoubi.
    I don't feel one bit of sorrow for him –
He had beaten and beaten and burned lit cigarettes
    into his ex-girlfriend's breasts and vagina
before strangling her.

    It occurred to me, the executed might lose the rights
to their body parts and become in-the-dark donors.
    Meaning, someone today might have the sicko's heart
inside them, keeping them alive and able to suck on tic tacs.
    The heart sends more messages to the brain
than the brain sends to the heart.

    A one-sided relationship, like the inmate
who writes his mother daily to report
    such things as: *We had oatmeal today*
with little dried flecks of apple in it
    and last night they gave us microwave popcorn
at group therapy – the theme being
    did you ever go to camp as a child?
But the mother writing back only sparingly –
    one birthday and one Christmas card each year.

The French stopped executing people in 1981.
    I stopped visiting the lockdown memory
care unit, where I read poems to those
    once on a trajectory to the sun
now vagrant, itinerant, hobo.
    Poems like Christina Rossetti's that asks:
Shall I meet other wayfarers at night?

A poem with the near-obsolete word: *hostler* –
which means a man who cares for horses
    especially at an inn.

And a woman in the memory unit, wearing a gray
    sweatshirt with food stains on it, saying
My sister with seventeen fractures –
    and all the horses came
and put their heads down close to her.

At home, we argue about whether or not
to have an exterminator come
    to eradicate the spiders with poisons.
Pleading for alternatives, I vacuum and broom away
    a myriad of webs; dust the windowsills
with talc powder in the scent of citrus –
    turn off the porch light.

I am buzzed into the memory care unit
    through the electronic security door
offering an option to Bingo and Judge Judy –
    bequeathing the sum of
something fanatical and jeweled.
    The tongue of the new man
is distended to many times its original size
    as if a long-tailed antelope squirrel
has been birthed inside his mouth.
    In an almost indecipherable language
he tells us his real home is on the
    Pine Ridge Reservation, where
he rode grass-eating horses all day and everywhere.
    And the poem ends:
But is there for the night a resting place?

NO ALPHABET

If not for the lust of women, there would be no alphabet.
Save for the breaking of traffic rules, there would be
no Cubism; no fractured light scrutinized from subways
or kaleidoscopes in the tool belts of surveyors.

Save for the white shoes the busgirl wore
there would be no cloud-colored shoe polish hardening
under the sink cabinet; no wet-chalk streaking
the sidewalk during the summer monsoons.

Save for the ravishing bruise stenciled across the man's cheek
there would be no hand-to-hand combat.
No 7-Eleven thieves with nylon stockings over their heads.
No trail marked with the shells of sunflower seeds
from the church steeple to the strip bar.

If not for his tiny, expensively coiffed gray-haired wife
the judge would never get out of bed.
Save for the lead saucepan of water in the dry grass
there would be no means to quench our thirst.
If not for the napoleons and éclairs the busgirl pilfered
from the walk-in cooler at the country club
she might not have been bulimic.

Save for the hearth rugs made from the skins of bears
placed in front of fireplaces lit with gas
falsifying every sighting of fallen stars seen
since the inception of love, there may never have
been application of kohl around women's eyes.
If not for the avarice for heated seats and more legroom
the average new car might not be weighing-in
at four-thousand and nine pounds.

And the stranger's car might have weighed just enough less
that my son's black and white wolf-dog, Santo,
might not be dead and my son would not have the dog
lying on snow in the back of his pickup, bringing it home to bury.

Save for a hollowed-out tree trunk, there would be
no place for the dead to reassemble their limbs.
Save for a shovel, there might not be a heaven.
No flowers thrown into prehistoric graves.
Save for the aura of light before a seizure
there would be no steel girders
to keep the sublime monsters
from entering the atmosphere of earth.

INVIDIA

I wake from a Dionysian dream with the headache of a diabetic
and a physical deformity born of jealousy –

and the sound of a large red-cheeked flicker
jack-hammering against the stucco

of what was once my ex-husband's workshop –
place of welded flames, litter of termite-infested lumber

that is now my low-to-the-ground tower
& place of jittered love. *Gelatinous* could be

the term for a certain type of jellied attachment
or a word to illustrate a curved breast or curdled milk.

But who would want to be the pale-skinned queen
inside a curtained carriage, hiding from the starving

and uproarious peasants staggering in the streets?
A friend named Anthony is going into the desert

to fast, so he can feel. No reason for rivalry.
I too could fast, if someone would chain me up

out of reach of cupboards and room service.
And though I only met my stepfather's mother once

I was gifted her gold necklace after she died.
No reason for following the convention

of donning black mourning clothes –
she lived into her nineties, swam every day

& was never in a camp.
Invidia is the Roman Goddess of Envy.

I am not envious of the poet whose husband built her a lap pool.
I am jealous of any woman my man brings pastries to.

I am envious of the life of a country vet and those
able to decline invitations to second bowls of soup.

Tony will come back from the desert
thin as a discounted pane of glass.

His wife will thicken him with
saltwater taffy and steamed new potatoes.

I am envious of those with devotional qualities.
And those whose cars have leather interiors.

I am jealous that there is such a thing as a corset muscle
and that someone is named Saturday.

I pretend not to, but I suffer a crippling
jealousy of the herd of white heifers

my man conceals in his backyard pen
and feeds roses and mushrooms to –

even though they can only stampede
upon him in the script of hooves.

DIALOGUE OF THE DEAF

A spray-painted and garmented dead tree is still a dead tree.
And conversing is as over-esteemed as Pythagoras' Theorem.
Though I understand he was born on an island
to an engraver of gems. Only the black and white photo
of a woman swimming underwater has meaning to me this morning.
And the most arresting image in last night's dream
was of a human flesh & blood baby
placed in the arms of a cardboard mother.
But let's not listen to the deipnosophist bloviate –
spewing long-winded and full-of-herself speeches.
Instead, look at the tarragon, the mustard greens
and the beets placed amorously on the plate
and the array of shoes under the table.

The wind is in remission today, and though my birthday
is months away, I want a book of paper dolls as a gift to
commemorate the day I came out of my mother's vagina.
You think I'm crude, others think I'm cured.
Not like a Spanish ham, but like a cripple
who can walk again after being touched
in the tent by a televangelist.
It's hard to believe I'm in love
with a man who loves Jimmy Swaggart –
who records his middle of the night telecasts
to watch later while ironing.

I would happily cut with small rubber-handled scissors
and fold the little cardboard tabs on the dresses
to adhere them to the nude and sexless paper body.

Still $a^2 + b^2 = c^2$
makes no impression in modeling clay
or in the interstitial islands located
between my ribs and tongue.
My head is tilted toward the assortment
of leather and jute under the table
as the Dialogue de sourds is racketing above.
The only words without counterfeit iridescence
are being spoken out the window near to the well
by widowers talking daily to their beloved deceaseds.
And the whisper into the ear of a stricken mule.

COLOR-RIDDEN

I get doped-up on color; my man gets doped-up on color.
A puppy-love of color is what we have in common.
      Like glue-sniffers adhered in an alley.

While he is motor scootering around Thailand, looking at tanned-legged women,
I go to the paint store – return with the darkest teal to sheath our bedroom walls.
And acquiesce that undergarments in hues of pale milk are elegiac.

The aura of a tarred and feathered person is black.
Black is the tuxedo on the torso of a groom.
Hard to gauge if the bride or the groom is more terror-stricken.

Let us not judge the bride for her breakfast of benzodiazepines.
Let the groom have a hard-on at the altar, whether it's for his

snow-cloaked, soon-to-be-wife, or for the showy light
coming through the rose-colored stained glass.

May they be equally elated   honeymooning in a high-rise by the sea
      as in a nylon tent pitched in wind-bedeviled dunes.

Let me not evict a pale bird from its nest of tangerine peels.
Nor call my man a *lowlife*.

Let me not care if I ever call him *husband*; nor forget he is colorblind.

Let the gossip be that we are hallowed ground.
I've kept our walls the color of ghost, in love's invisible honor.

Let us not pray for a villa in Croatia
or to ride in a red convertible wearing a tiara.

Unable to wave off the scavenger birds;
let us not dissipate any more of God's delirium.

INSIDE THE JIVA OF A MADWOMAN

"I'd rather be in the mountains thinking of God, than in church thinking about the mountains."

- John Muir

Rather be walking in plastic high heels through a sunless tunnel
than be inside a pine coffin in the back of a wagon in a Faulkner novel.

Rather be chugging flat champagne or three-day-old bone broth
than talking on the phone to a psychic in Aurora, Colorado.

Rather be wet inside a ripped blue raincoat
than be the subject inside a black velvet painting.

Rather be handcuffed to a sanitation worker than a nun.
Unless she saw visons.

Yet, more and more, the thorns of goat head weeds infect my blood
as I somersault for a camera that is only pretending to film my acrobatic body.

On a near-dusk winter day, I watch a woman in a full-length black mink coat
and a black mink hat walk down a lane that once hosted the hooves of sheep.

Her waist is as cylindrical as a crayon or a test tube.

Rather be a four-pawed black mink in a burrow on the banks of an icy river.

Cryophobia is the fear of cold.

Rather sing tonelessly on the Grand Ole Opry stage than sing to a child in a coma.

In the next world, we will be babied, believed to lack
the capacity for servitude or revolution.

Appropriating a spelling bee, a blue goddess, an accordion player
cantillating songs about a world in which we all have access

to transmigration and transatlantic cruises;
vocal chords and haloes of buttercups.

DECLINE IN THE ADORATION OF JACK-IN-THE-PULPITS

The bijou Jack-in-the-Pulpit plant
looks like it's kneeling in dirt on tiny dragon
knees in comparative darkness - and conjures
a frocked man propagandizing at an altar.
If ingested raw, its hooded bloom is poison.
Even so, it's a part of paradise that won't survive behind glass.
What happens will go down in history as fable.

No one takes baths in the placid dark anymore.
There are too few hatmakers left.
Almost no silence to be found.
The days are sad and many people's backs hurt.
We are too occupied with our devices to notice
         what is crescendoing in the woods.

Cell phones are like bird coffins in our hands.
No one makes love without a mirror or a camera to witness –
         often the sounds are recorded.
No one gets injured without posting pictures of the wound,
the veering drive to urgent care, the forlorn face of the nurse
practitioner sewing the stitches, the hot dog eaten afterward.

What is this ceaseless self-focus, but the hoopla,
         hue, and cry of an un-held baby?
A harelip never tended with a floral unguent.
No rain or sun on our skin, only the hum and haloes
of screens swaddling us.

         So, when an angelic transvestite in powder
blue hot pants and lustrous violet butterfly wings approaches
on the avenue with an offer of a piece of her soul
along with a piece of *Dulce de Leche* ice cream pie
and a shot of pink-tinted tequila,

we are too vanished inside
a dull vortex, looking at facsimiles of flowers, fountains & females
to invite her inside and massage her exquisite feet.
    Instead, we become frantic and apoplectic to find that we've lost
our chargers and it's 3:17 am and the Apple Store is closed.

And we don't notice the twenty-four carat
        cut-adrift-angel
    walking away on black pavement
        swaying her veritable ass –
    ferrying her gifts out of reach.

POST SCRIPTUM: I DON'T DRIVE TRACTORS

You and I, recherché reader, have grown older, but we never got tattooed
on a Navy ship, or in a prison cell, or in a chic boutique parlor –

therefore, we don't have to get the magnum opuses lasered off now
in time for death. Though, if we did have violet-throated herons

tatted along our thighs, dragons giving birth to other dragons
on the smalls of our backs, or angels with orchids in their mouths

on the expanding flesh of our abdomens –
who would know once we are lying in our coffins?

Not much skin is left exposed in the campo of a coffin.
Men are donned in dry-cleaned or cologne-spritzed suits

and women in special-occasion dresses.
I hope not to be wearing a moth-balled double-breasted suit

or a tangerine-colored chiffon dress in the style
of a woman standing on the deck of a cruise ship at dusk.

Nor, with any luck, will they wrap me up
in a black plastic Hefty bag –

the kind used as curtains on West San Francisco St.
where I lived for a time with Scott and Scott, who

let me sleep on the floor in an alcove adjacent to their kitchen –
in the closest dimensions to a cell that I have ever slept in

without feeling immured. It was suitable in my early
twenties to sleep in my sleeping bag on someone else's

grey linoleum, near the trash bins – pay no rent
and wear silver spray-painted cowboy boots.

Decades later, I cohabitate with a gamophobic psychologist
who also does not charge me rent and I get to sleep in a bed.

Sometimes I do domestic chores and sometimes I don't.
He wants me to learn to drive his tractor

but I decline. For too much sitting leads to
restless leg syndrome and depersonalization disorder.

It's hard to believe he wasn't taught that.
But he did educate me about the perils of triangles.

That is why I won't be buried in the same hole with him
and his sister, any of his ex-fiancés, or ex-favorite patients.

And since he and I don't have symbols on our skin to convey
our stories to the next world; and he has a disaffinity for

lamenting crickets and weeping women inside his home,
and we can't rely on hymnals or ringed fingers –

I order myself an eyelash-growing drug from India
and for him, the DVD *Alone in the Wilderness.*

RIDING WITH NO HANDS

There must be a reason why a man rides his bike with no hands.
Why charismatic cult leaders like fountain pens and small Asian
women walking on their backs.
Why religions assign more significance to the soul than the body.
There must be a reason why no one cancels their appointment
with the palm reader Rosa.
Reasons a young man trades sexual favors for rusted shoe buckles.
And why we reward obedience over amorous abandon.
At twelve I fell off my bike and broke my collarbone.
As I lay at the bottom of the hill on black-tarred pavement
there were people all around me, but no one to say
mi preciosa, you are but a bruised flower.
I could push rewind and return to the womb.
There must be a reason I don't want to.

My pregnant mother had long legs and smoked unfiltered cigarettes
as she walked by the sea. Ate bratwurst with onions and relish
and drank bottles of Yoo-hoo as she walked by the sea.
There must be a reason why the adorned body
is both coveted & scorned; hankered after & ridiculed
like the fluctuating sentiments directed toward a decorated soldier
just back from war. Smoked and walked by the sea,
overturning horseshoe crabs and collecting beach glass.

There must be a reason that our dogs don't hightail it away

from us into the hills and form their own colonies.

A reason the words trigger and happy are paired.

Rosa reads palms in the room with saint statues and dark magenta walls

as her children and mother cut out paper dolls one room over.

There must be a reason why Purgatory no longer exists.

And children swallow coins.

A reason we ask for separate checks and separate exits.

And prefer not to lend our hairbrushes.

A reason why we are infatuated with ululating ghosts.

GRACIAS, ANSELMO

For the exquisite peacock carved on your gate.

For the tea and ghee-buttered toast you deliver to me in bed.

My sickness is that of *grasping and aversion*; it circles like an ailing

white crane above my lungs. Thank you for not spanking me

for coloring outside of the lines. And for fostering my illusion

that love can survive a plummet down the side of a mountain.

Thank you for not laughing at me as I drove away in a blue van

with bald tires and three men wearing papier-mâché masks.

Thank you for the cooing sounds of the mourning dove.

They say the melancholic birds are monogamous

which makes their sadness even more confusing.

The borders between birds and us are not real.

Just like any curtain can be pulled back and any glue can un-adhere.

So, let's go listen to Mariachi music.

Prostrate on the ground in gratitude to the animal before eating it.

Thank the unknown sheep as we thank the Unknown Soldier.

Thank the molecules that make morphine.

Starry-eyed and purring.

Thank you for polishing your shoes for the wedding.

Thank you for hanging paintings of horses on my walls.

For letting me go to the Shiva temple alone

though I thought a lot about you while I was there

and again, later when I saw the dirt on the bottoms of my feet.

Thank you for the black hyacinthine in your hand

and for being a strong carrier of stones.

For not making too much of how easily I cry.

For being my unsparing destroyer.

ACKNOWLEDGMENTS

Grateful acknowledgment is given to the editors of the publications in which the following poems first appeared:

The American Poetry Review: *Levels of Lead; Shining Bucket; So, You Think I'm Afraid of You?; Tarzan Aubade*

Best American Poetry 2019: *Decline in the Adoration of Jack-in-the-Pulpits*

Conduit: *Cult of the White Bear; Handsome Is as Handsome Does; Riding with No Hands*

The Common: *No Alphabet*

Copper Nickel: *Semi-Jubilant Conversion Song*

Florida Review: *Seven Valleys*

The Kenyon Review: *Decline in the Adoration of Jack-in-the-Pulpits*

The Massachusetts Review: *Trajectory to the Sun*

The New England Review: *Dialogue of the Deaf; Lead in the Boots of the Messengers; Patron of Embalmers*

New Ohio Review: *Miracle of Life; Shallow Person*

Poetry City USA: *Re-entry*

Shadowgraph: *Autostrada of the Lakes; Gracias, Anselmo*

Southword: *When Almonds Appear in Dreams- shortlisted for the Gregory O'Donoghue International Poetry Prize 2017*

Gratitude to the following people and organizations
for their seen & unseen influences on the poems in *Rasa*;
for both holding me up and pushing me into the storm:

David Lehman, Susan Terris, Marsh Hawk Press.
Helen Hurley, Juliana Young, Tony Hoagland.
Nodiah Brent, Heidi Cost, Lindsay Ahl, Christine McCarthy.
Dana Levin, Dean Young, Elizabeth Scanlon, Ellen Dore Watson.
James Thomas Stevens, Danny Solis, Gabrielle Viethen.
James Dwyer, William Dwyer, David Dwyer, Justin Young.
Rona Jaffe Foundation, Witter Bynner Foundation,
Sarabande Books, Warren Wilson's Program for Writers.
August Young, Paige Young, Anselmo Gallegos.